◉ Smithsonian

The Secrets of MERCURY

by Emma Carlson Berne

CAPSTONE PRESS
a capstone imprint

Capstone Press
1710 Roe Crest Drive, North Mankato, Minnesota 56003
www.capstonepub.com

Library of Congress Cataloging-in-Publication Data
Berne, Emma Carlson, author.
 The secrets of Mercury / by Emma Carlson Berne.
   pages cm. — (Smithsonian. Planets)
 Summary: "Discusses the planet Mercury, including observations by ancient cultures, current knowledge of Mercury, and plans for future scientific research and space exploration"—Provided by publisher.
 Audience: Ages 8-10
 Audience: Grades 2 to 4
 ISBN 978-1-4914-5866-2 (library binding)
 ISBN 978-1-4914-5899-0 (paperback)
 ISBN 978-1-4914-5910-2 (eBook PDF)
1. Mercury (Planet)—Juvenile literature. 2. Mercury (Planet)—Exploration—Juvenile literature. I. Title.
 QB611.B47 2016
 523.41—dc23   2014046196

Editorial Credits
Elizabeth R. Johnson, editor; Tracy Davies McCabe and Kazuko Collins, designers;
Wanda Winch, media researcher; Tori Abraham, production specialist

Our very special thanks to Andrew K. Johnston, Geographer, Center for Earth and Planetary Studies, National Air and Space Museum, Smithsonian Institution, for his curatorial review. Capstone would also like to thank Kealy Gordon, Smithsonian Institution Product Development Manager, and the following at Smithsonian Enterprises: Ellen Nanney, Licensing Manager; Brigid Ferraro, Director of Licensing; Carol LeBlanc, Senior Vice President, Consumer & Education Products; Chris Liedel, President.

Photo Credits
Black Cat Studios: Ron Miller, 13, 17 (bottom), 27 (top); Capstone, 7 (middle); European Space Agency, 19 (b), 29; Lunar and Planetary Institute, 5 (b); NASA: Johns Hopkins University Applied Physics Laboratory/Carnegie Institution of Washington, cover, back cover, 1, 5 (back), 15 (all), 17 (top left), 23, 25, JPL, 21, JPL/Northwestern University, 20; National Air and Space Museum, Smithsonian Institution, 22; National Geographic Creative: Chris Foss, 17 (top right); Newscom: UPI/Bill Ingalls, 27 (b); Rijksmuseum, Amsterdam, 7 (bl); Science Source: Chris Butler, 11, Detlev van Ravenswaay, 19 (t); Shutterstock: Aleksandar Todorovic, 7 (br), Bildagentur Zoonar GmbH, space background, Vladimir Zadvinski, 7 (tr); Thinkstock: Photos.com, 9 (all); Wikipedia: Alexander von Humboldt, 7 (tl)

Direct Quotations
Page 27 from NASA Solar System Exploration profile, solarsystem.nasa.gov/people/

Table of Contents

First Rock from the Sun

In the vastness of space, a small, rocky planet spins. It twirls alone, without a moon, baking in the burning heat of the Sun.

The planets in our solar system can be divided into two groups: inner planets and outer planets. Mercury is an inner planet, like Venus, Earth, and Mars. These planets are closer to the Sun and are made of rock and metal. Farther from the Sun, the outer planets are gas giants. They are Jupiter, Saturn, Uranus, and Neptune.

Mercury is the smallest planet in our solar system. It is only slightly larger than Earth's moon. It is also the planet closest to the Sun. Only two space missions have explored this planet. Why is that? The Sun helps Mercury keep its secrets. Even though they are 36 million miles (58 million kilometers) apart, the Sun's heat and gravity are so powerful that exploring Mercury is very difficult to do.

Mercury and Venus are the only planets in the solar system that do not have moons.

Fast Facts

Distance from Sun: 36 million miles
(58 million km)

Diameter: 3,032 miles
(4,879 km)

Moons: 0

Rings: 0

Length of day: 59 Earth days

Length of year: 88 Earth days

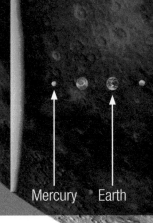

Mercury   Earth

Mythology of Mercury

Just like today, the world's ancient peoples charted and studied the movements of stars and planets.

The Mayans recorded Mercury's movements in detail. The Egyptians called Mercury Thoth, the god of knowledge. The early people of Northern Europe referred to Mercury as Odin, the god of wisdom, magic, and war. Ancient peoples in India referred to Mercury as the god Budha.

The Romans noted that this small planet traveled quickly across the sky. They named it after their god of trade and travel. Mercury was a messenger who wore winged sandals.

The earliest discovered record of Mercury's presence was written in Mesopotamia, dating from 265 BC.

Ancient Greeks thought Mercury was two planets, because they saw it in the evening sky and then again in the morning sky. The planet was not visible later in the night because it is so close to the Sun. It is often below the nighttime horizon. Other times only the side of Mercury in shadow faces Earth, making it appear invisible to us.

Mercury

Mayan records

Thoth

Odin

Budha

7

Discovering Mercury

In the early 1700s, astronomers such as Galileo Galilei were able to observe Mercury through their telescopes. The planet appeared as a small gray disc. Later more powerful telescopes suggested that Mercury had a moonlike surface. Beyond this, everything else about the planet was a mystery.

small size means its gravity isn't
g. Because Mercury is so close to
ny spacecraft that goes to Mercury
lled away by the Sun's powerful
is very difficult to keep a spacecraft
y's orbit.

In modern times there have been more than 20 successful missions to Mars. But only two have gone to Mercury. In 1974 the Mariner 10 spacecraft made the journey to the first planet. Finally scientists had a good look at the surface of Mercury.

The MESSENGER spacecraft was also sent to Mercury in 2004. It spent more than 10 years in space, and more than 4 years in orbit around Mercury before ts impact with the surface of the planet.

Galileo demonstrates his telescope

Galileo, who lived in 16th century Italy, is one of the most important astronomers in history. He improved the telescopes used at the time. He made discoveries about Mercury, Venus, and the moons of Jupiter. He also believed that Earth moved around the Sun. At the time, it was commonly believed that the Sun moved around Earth. Some people call Galileo "the father of modern science."

A Nearly Absent Atmosphere

Earth's atmosphere protects us from solar radiation and gives us air to breathe. Venus' thick atmosphere is hot as an oven and filled with poisonous gases. But Mercury has very little atmosphere at all.

Instead, Mercury has a thin layer of atoms called an exosphere. This layer is constantly blasted by a stream of tiny particles from the Sun. When this solar wind interacts with Mercury's magnetic field, twisting magnetic zones can form. These invisible tornadoes can be 500 miles (805 km) wide, sometimes reaching the planet's surface and releasing atoms into the exosphere.

Mercury's atmosphere is made up of sodium, hydrogen, and oxygen. But it has nowhere near enough oxygen to breathe.

Mercury has the thinnest atmosphere of all the planets in our solar system.

What's the Weather?

Rain? Wind? Clouds? Nope. Mercury doesn't have much weather at all. Weather happens in an atmosphere. Earth, for instance, has a thick atmosphere with many different kinds of weather. But because Mercury has hardly any atmosphere, it has no moisture, no wind, no storms, and no clouds.

Since Mercury is so close to the Sun, you would think it would be extremely hot—and it is during the day. Daytime temperatures on the surface can reach 800 degrees Fahrenheit (427 °Celsius). But there is almost no atmosphere to hold in that heat. The nights very quickly plunge more than 1,000 degrees to as low as -290 °F (-179 °C).

PLANET	High Temperatures	Low Temperatures	Range
Earth	134 °F (57 °C)	-135 °F (-93 °C)	269 °F (150 °C)
Mercury	800 °F (427 °C)	-290 °F (-179 °C)	1,090 °F (606 °C)

Mercury

When it faces the Sun, Mercury's surface is hot enough to melt some metals.

If You Were Standing on Mercury

Take an imaginary spaceship and land it on Mercury. Open the hatch and step out. At first glance the landscape is very similar to the Moon. Mercury's surface is dark gray, bare, and rocky. But *unlike* the Moon, the planet is also studded with giant valleys and cliffs, bigger than those found on Earth.

Look up at Mercury's sky. The Sun looks huge! On the surface of Mercury, the Sun looks three times bigger than it does on Earth. You're a lot closer now. Wait for night. Now, examine the stars. They appear to hardly move at all. Although Mercury moves rapidly around the Sun, it spins on its axis rather slowly. It takes Mercury about 59 Earth days to spin just once.

Astronomers used to think that Mercury was tidally locked with the Sun. That would mean the same side of Mercury always faced the Sun, the same way the Moon is tidally locked to Earth. The secret of Mercury's rotation was uncovered in 1965. It's not tidally locked after all.

Scientists have called one strange formation on Mercury "The Spider."

It has more than 100 flat channels radiating out from a central crater.

The Secrets of Mercury's Craters and Cliffs

Asteroids are constantly showering the inner planets. Most of the time, they burn up in the planets' protective atmospheres. Because Mercury has almost no atmosphere, asteroids crash right into its surface. This creates a lot of craters, big and small.

Mercury also has an amazing number of cliffs and valleys. The cliffs are called scarps. Some of these scarps are tens of miles long, and up to a mile high. No other planet in the solar system has so many cliffs. Scientists think Mercury's cliffs were created because the planet was hot when it was formed. Mercury shrank as it cooled. The surface contracted and buckled, creating the cliffs and valleys.

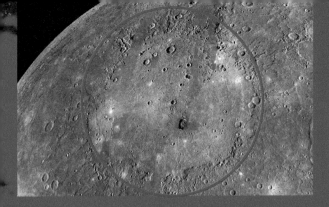

The Caloris Basin on Mercury is almost 960 miles (1,545 km) across. By comparison, the Vredefort crater in South Africa—the biggest visible crater on Earth—is only 186 miles (299 km) across.

Scientists think an asteroid impact made the Caloris Basin crater billions of years ago. The asteroid was likely larger than 62 miles (100 km) across. That's about as wide as the state of Connecticut.

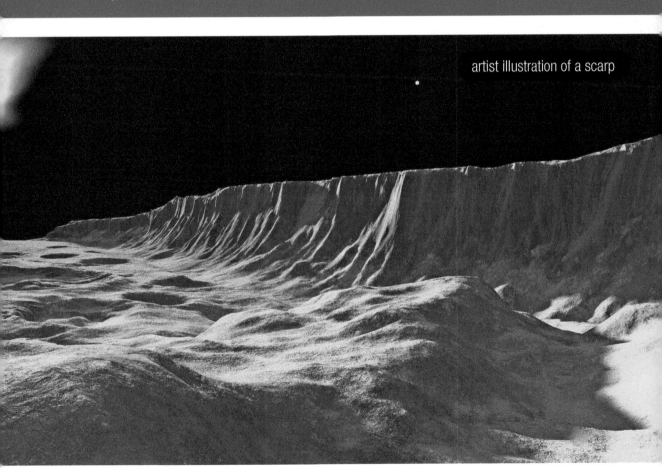

artist illustration of a scarp

Odd Orbit

Mercury's orbit around the Sun is oddly shaped. Most planet orbits are almost circular. But Mercury goes around the Sun in a more oval-shaped pattern. Mercury also wobbles a little as it orbits.

This wobble makes for a strange effect on the sunrise and sunset on Mercury. If you were to watch the sunrise, you would see the Sun rise over the horizon, then set briefly, then rise again! At sunset the reverse would happen. The Sun would appear to set, then rise, then set again. Imagine how surprised you would be if that happened on Earth!

How far do the planets travel in their orbit?

PLANET	DISTANCE TRAVELED
Mercury	223.7 million miles (360 million km)
Earth	584 million miles (940 million km)
Neptune	17.5 billion miles (28 billion km)

Scientists theorize that Mercury's wobbly orbit may be the result of getting smacked with a huge asteroid long ago.

artist illustration of Mercury's surface

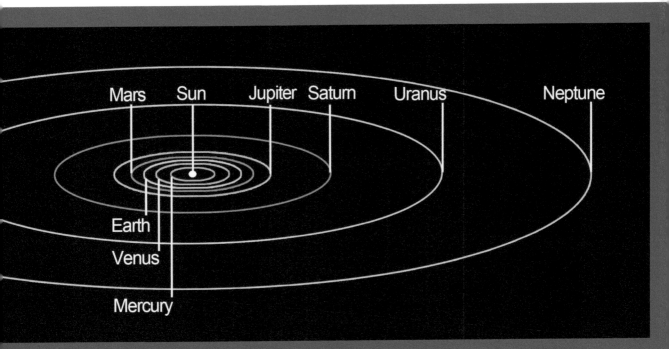

Mars Sun Jupiter Saturn Uranus Neptune

Earth

Venus

Mercury

Mariner 10: The Beginning

Before the 1970s scientists had barely explored Mercury at all. The planet next to the Sun was wrapped in secrets. But all of that changed when the Mariner 10 spacecraft was sent to investigate it.

As Mariner 10 blasted out of Earth's atmosphere and into space, it turned and snapped photos of our planet and moon. Mariner 10's cameras sent back photos with high-resolution digital color. Photos of Earth and the Moon were combined to create this famous image of the Earth-Moon system.

Mariner 10 launched in November 1973. With its solar panels expanded, it was about 26 feet (8 meters) across. Mariner 10 used these panels to gather the power it needed from the light of the Sun. The spacecraft took 16 months to reach its destination.

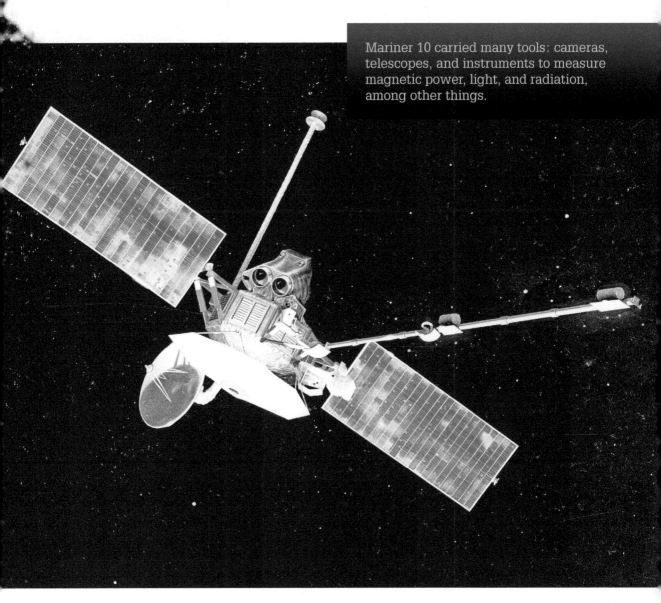

Mariner 10 carried many tools: cameras, telescopes, and instruments to measure magnetic power, light, and radiation, among other things.

Mariner 10: The Successful Mission

The robotic Mariner 10 spacecraft first flew toward Venus. It used Venus' gravity to slingshot closer to Mercury. This "gravity-assist" allowed the spacecraft to change its speed and flight path so that it could reach Mercury.

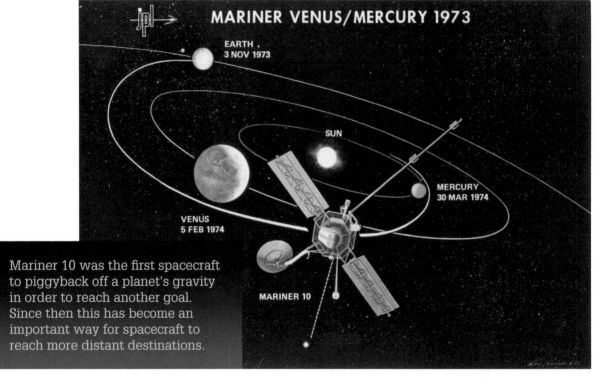

MARINER VENUS/MERCURY 1973

EARTH
3 NOV 1973

SUN

MERCURY
30 MAR 1974

VENUS
5 FEB 1974

MARINER 10

Mariner 10 was the first spacecraft to piggyback off a planet's gravity in order to reach another goal. Since then this has become an important way for spacecraft to reach more distant destinations.

illustration of Mariner 10 flying by Mercury

Mariner 10 saw the same side of Mercury on each of its three flybys. The other half of the planet was still a mystery for many years.

The sturdy Mariner 10 flew by Mercury three times in 1974 and 1975. The spacecraft sent photographs back to scientists watching from Earth.

Scientists could finally get a good look at the surface of Mercury. They saw the huge cliffs and craters that mark the planet's surface for the first time. In total, Mariner 10 took more than 7,000 images. It successfully mapped about 40 percent of Mercury's surface.

MESSENGER: A Deeper Look

Another spacecraft was sent on a mission to Mercury in 2004: MESSENGER. Mariner 10 sent back never-before-seen pictures. But MESSENGER would finally give scientists a complete look at Mercury.

Before locking onto Mercury's orbit in 2011, MESSENGER had a long journey. It flew through the inner solar system in an uneven spiral pattern. MESSENGER circled the Sun 15 times before its official arrival. Why? MESSENGER used flybys of Earth, Venus, and Mercury to get gravity-assists. This plan adjusted the path and speed of the spacecraft, saving fuel. The extra-long journey made the mission possible with the rockets available.

In its first 10 years in space, MESSENGER made 29 trips around the Sun, orbited Mercury more than 3,000 times, and sent more than 250,000 images back to Earth. Mercury's entire surface has now been mapped.

MESSENGER wore a ceramic cloth sunshade to protect it from the nearby Sun's blistering heat.

Mirrors on MESSENGER's solar panels reflected some sunlight away from the spacecraft, so it wouldn't overheat.

MESSENGER stands for MErcury Surface, Space ENvironment, GEochemistry, and Ranging.

MESSENGER: Uncovering Mercury's Secrets

MESSENGER has shown scientists that Mercury is more complex than they thought. Scientists used to think volcanoes might be impossible on Mercury. But MESSENGER found proof that huge volcanic vents spewed hot lava onto Mercury's surface. The lava blasted through the surface rock and shaped the planet's valleys.

Using data about Mercury's gravity field, landscape, and spin, MESSENGER also discovered that Mercury has a huge internal core. The core is about 75 percent of the entire diameter of the planet. This is the largest internal core, percentage-wise, of all the known planets.

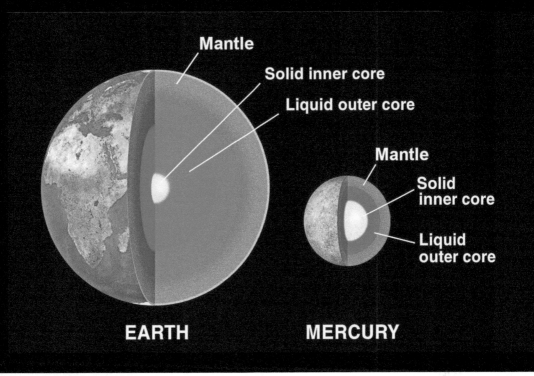

Mantle
Solid inner core
Liquid outer core

Mantle
Solid inner core
Liquid outer core

EARTH   MERCURY

Scientist Spotlight: Louise Prockter

Growing up in England, Louise Prockter never thought that one day she would work on missions to space. But as the supervisor of the Planetary Exploration Group at Johns Hopkins' Applied Physics Laboratory, she does just that. Prockter has studied images from Jupiter's moon Ganymede and studied photos of an asteroid called Eros. She learned all about delicate, complicated spacecraft tools while working on the MESSENGER mission. Prockter remembers seeing MESSENGER's first pictures of the previously unseen side of Mercury. "I was so thrilled that the image was perfect, and so relieved that it was exactly in the center of the field of view, as we had planned it!"

Mercury and the Future

Rocky, sun-scorched Mercury still has secrets to share with Earth's scientists. Signs of frozen water were found in the bottom of craters in October 2014. These north pole craters are always shadowed from sunlight, which kept this secret hidden for many years. Now scientists are trying to discover how the ice may have arrived on Mercury. It's possible that it traveled on a comet that crashed into the planet. They also want to find out if the ice is billions of years old or far more recent.

In 2017 the European Space Agency hopes to launch the BepiColombo mission: two spacecraft that will fly to Mercury. With the extreme difficulties of studying Mercury, we cannot know if the BepiColombo mission will succeed. But one thing is for sure—exploration of our solar system will continue. We have many questions, and little Mercury has lots of answers for us to uncover.

By studying how water arrived on Mercury, scientists may learn how water is delivered to all planets, including Earth.

BepiColombo Mission Goals:

- Analyze the materials that make up Mercury
- Measure Mercury's magnetic field
- Figure out if Mercury's huge inner core is molten or solid

29

Glossary

asteroid (AS-tuh-royd)—a small rocky body that orbits the Sun

astronomy (uh-STRAH-nuh-mee)—the study of stars, planets, and space

atmosphere (AT-muhss-fihr)—the mixture of gases that surrounds a planet or moon

axis (AK-siss)—an imaginary line through the middle of an object, around which that object spins

contract (Kuhn-TRAKT)—to become smaller

crater (KRAY-tuhr)—a large hole in the ground caused by something such as a bomb or meteorite

diameter (dye-AM-uh-tur)—a straight line through the center of a circle, from one side to another

gas giant—large planets such as Jupiter, Saturn, Uranus, and Neptune that are made mostly of gas, without a solid surface

gravity (GRAV-uh-tee)—the force that pulls things down or to the center of a planet and keeps them from floating away into space

magnetic field (mag-NEH-tik)—an area of magnetic force around a large object like a planet

Mesopotamia (meh-so-poh-TAY-mee-uh)—an area in southwestern Asia between the Tigris and Euphrates rivers, in what is now Iraq; called the "cradle of civilization"

molten (MOHLT-uhn)—melted by heat; lava is molten rock

orbit (OR-bit)—the invisible path followed by an object circling a planet, the Sun, etc.

radiation (RAY-dee-AY-shuhn)—energy that comes from a source in the form of waves or rays that you cannot see; radiation can be dangerous energy

robot (ROH-bot)—a machine that is programmed to do jobs that are usually performed by a person

solar wind (SOH-lur)—a stream of particles released from the Sun

Read More

Aguilar, David. *Space Encyclopedia: A Tour of Our Solar System and Beyond.* Washington D.C.: National Geographic, 2013.

Carney, Elizabeth. *National Geographic Readers: Planets.* Washington D.C.: National Geographic, 2012.

Nardo, Don. *Destined for Space: Our Story of Exploration.* Mankato, Minn: Capstone Press, 2012.

Internet Sites

FactHound offers a safe, fun way to find Internet sites related to this book. All of the sites on FactHound have been researched by our staff.

Here's all you do:

Visit *www.facthound.com*

Type in this code: 9781491458662

Check out projects, games and lots more at
www.capstonekids.com

Critical Thinking Using the Common Core

1. Why does Mercury's location near the Sun make it difficult for spacecraft to study the planet? (Key Ideas and Details)

2. Look at the table on page 12. Why does Mercury have a bigger temperature range than Earth? If scientists were going to land a spacecraft on Mercury, why would they have to think about the temperature range? (Integration of Knowledge and Ideas)

Index